94461
ACP-6217

D1468507

MAY   2004

silent k as in knot

Carey Molter

Consulting Editor Monica Marx, M.A./Reading Specialist

ABDO Publishing Company

Published by SandCastle™, an imprint of ABDO Publishing Company, 4940 Viking Drive, Edina, Minnesota 55435.

Printed in the United States.

Credits
Edited by: Pam Price
Curriculum Coordinator: Nancy Tuminelly
Cover and Interior Design and Production: Mighty Media
Photo Credits: Comstock, Creatas, Hemera, PhotoDisc, Stockbyte

Library of Congress Cataloging-in-Publication Data

Molter, Carey, 1973-
    Silent K as in knot / Carey Molter.
        p. cm. -- (Silent letters)
    Includes index.
    Summary: Easy-to-read sentences introduce words that contain a silent "K," such as knot, knit, and knee.
    ISBN 1-59197-446-1
    1. English language--Consonants--Juvenile literature. [1. English language--Consonants.]
I. Title.

PE1159.M656 2003
428.1--dc21

                                                                2003048126

SandCastle™ books are created by a professional team of educators, reading specialists, and content developers around five essential components that include phonemic awareness, phonics, vocabulary, text comprehension, and fluency. All books are written, reviewed, and leveled for guided reading, early intervention reading, and Accelerated Reader® programs and designed for use in shared, guided, and independent reading and writing activities to support a balanced approach to literacy instruction.

Let Us Know

After reading the book, SandCastle would like you to tell us your stories about reading. What is your favorite page? Was there something hard that you needed help with? Share the ups and downs of learning to read. We want to hear from you! To get posted on the ABDO Publishing Company Web site, send us e-mail at:

sandcastle@abdopub.com

SandCastle Level: Beginning

Silent-k Words

knees

knife

knit

knob

knot

knuckles

3

Adam ties a knot
in the rope.

Uncle Leo cut the cake with a knife.

Knuckles are the joints in each finger.

Nina rests
her chin
on her knees.

Jen's grandma knit this hat and scarf for her.

The **knob** turns the machine on and off.

The Knight
Who Could Knit
Knots

There once was a knight
who could knit knots.

He kept his yarn near his cot.

At night he would
kneel by the fire.

He'd knit very late and not tire.

At the sound of a knock he would stop.

The knight then gave
the new knot to his pop!

More Silent-k Words

knack

knave

knead

knickers

knickknack

knoll

knotty

know

knowledge

known

Glossary

cot   a small bed that can be folded up

kneel   to rest on your knees

knight   in ancient times, a warrior who wore a suit of armor and fought on horseback

knit   to make clothing or blankets using yarn and long, pointed needles

knob   a small handle that turns a device on or off

knot   the fastening made by tying one or more pieces of rope or string together

yarn   a long strand made up of fibers twisted together

About SandCastle™

A professional team of educators, reading specialists, and content developers created the SandCastle™ series to support young readers as they develop reading skills and strategies and increase their general knowledge. The SandCastle™ series has four levels that correspond to early literacy development in young children. The levels are provided to help teachers and parents select the appropriate books for young readers.

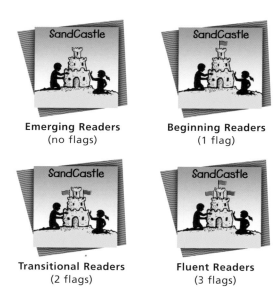

Emerging Readers
(no flags)

Beginning Readers
(1 flag)

Transitional Readers
(2 flags)

Fluent Readers
(3 flags)

These levels are meant only as a guide. All levels are subject to change.

To see a complete list of SandCastle™ books and other nonfiction titles from ABDO Publishing Company, visit www.abdopub.com or contact us at:

4940 Viking Drive, Edina, Minnesota 55435 • 1-800-800-1312 • fax: 1-952-831-1632